Spill That Fkn Ink White Girl

Alice White

BookLeaf Publishing

India | USA | UK

Presentation by *BookLeaf Publishing*

Web: www.bookleafpub.com

E-mail: info@bookleafpub.com

ISBN: 9789360943042

First edition 2024

DEDICATION

This book is dedicated
To: You, the reader,
From: Me, the writer!.
I hope you find what you are lookin'
for in the pages of this book or the
next one ... & if you don't, keep
searchin' til you do!.
Never Give Up ...

EVER ... eVeR ... ever ...

.7.3.1.5.7.4.4.0.7.2.   < - - - - - - - - ...I.C.E...

text me ... reach out ....

ACKNOWLEDGEMENT

I would like to thank BookLeaf Publishing & #TheWriteChallenge for their assistance in making my writings become a published possibility!. Both have been inspirational & motivational in this entire process.. An avenue was provided To: Me, the writer, From: Them, the publisher, for my thoughts, my feelings, & my ideas to be available to you & that is Absolutely Amazing in itself!.

I would also like to thank my entire family for sticking around to hear me out & continuing to love me through alllll the bullshit, as I know they had a choice.. A big thank you to our friends that made the decision to love us both in lieu of judgin' us, as I know they also had a choice..

I Thank You ALLLLL . . . from the inside of my dark, colorful heart, soul, & mind!.

PREFACE

Every written word you find in this book was written from the perspective of a loyal, dedicated wife, that somehow, some way, left a door open for another man to come into her life & take her away from her family.. The feelings this man stirred inside her were unlike anything she'd ever felt before . . . ever!. What was it?. Fate?. Infatuation?. Just her being stoopid?. Limerence?. Love?. IDK & she didn't either!. What you will find here are her thoughts & feelings for her husband, for herself, & for her life..

Spilled Ink

In the silence of my thoughts,
a torrent of words awaits..
A cascade of emotions,
a narrative that resonates..

Allow me to articulate
the depths within this heart..
Unveiling tales of trust & truth,
as this unheard of journey starts..

A life made up of turning twists
& then those twisting turns..
Not knowing of support right now,
my fkn spirit yearns..

Take a moment, this moment here,
settle into this space..
For the 'not so easy' path ahead,
is not your simple race..

In your own chaos find comfort,
take it, make it your own..
Together we'll navigate through
the seeds that have been sown..

Join me on this roller coaster,

a tumultuous ride..
With every turn & alllll the twists,
we'll just step & stride..

Relax & sink with me,
in tales that will now unfold..
As my thoughts turn right into words,
& are courageously told..

Your presence here brings a quiet peace,
a comforting touch..
In this chaotic song we sing,
you mean to me so much..

Laughter may dance dirty,
tears may unwillingly flow..
In written words thrown back & forth,
erotic emotions may grow..

So here & now we find ourselves,
on this journey into thought..
Into the foggy road ahead,
together we've been brought..

This canvas was once nothing,
it is now completely filled..
As alllll my mind's expressions can be found
in the ink that's been spilled . . .

11102023.01162024

Expected

I am the betrayer, I fkd it alllll up..
I'm now the one expected to fill your cup..

Smile & smile & do as you're told..
Step into character, play the role..

It's you & you & only you..
Everything else is not alllll true..

Your feelings are what led you here..
Your feelings, hmmm . . . should they be
feared..

Just smile & smile, fkn smile some more..
Like nothing of you anymore..

Maybe, just maybe, this will alllll come to
pass..
As we were alllll waiting, I was expected to
be stained glass..

10252023.01172024

Where Do You Live?

Where do you live?.
In my head, my hard head..

Why do you live there?.
For the dread, the dreaded dread..

What does that do?.
Well, I will tell you exactly what it does . . .
. . . it keeps me in bed..

When do you leave?.
Never, I plead..

Why do you choose to live in your head?.
It's not a choice but a curse for alllll that
bleed red..

10292023.01172024

Trust No One

No wonder trust no one..
No one under the sun..
Lies are told for fun..
The lies have just begun..

You only get one run..
You'll fuck it up a ton..
Wise wicked webs are spun..
Before the black widow is done..

So be careful out there, hon..
Someone's under the gun..
May feel their life is done..
Looking for you's to shun..

Trust will shock & stun..
You must start with none..
Zero, this isn't a pun..
You're now the winner ... you've won..

11162023.01172024

The Only Way Out Is Through

The only way out is through..
Thought everybody knew..
Today you're blue, we were once tooo,
Keep going, find a clue..

What once was is now not..
Let go of what you thought..
It's not forgot, you took the shot,
Keep going, it's a lot..

Walk, run, skip, or crawl..
Just go through it alllll..
You may fall, may hit a wall,
Keep going & stand tall..

Yourself, you're bound to find..
May even lose your mind..
You'll fall behind, just be kind,
Keep going, you will align..

One day you'll find a bend..
On this journey to amend..
It's not pretend, just comprehend,
Keep going, til the end..

11152023

Some Days

Rough chapter some say..
Everybody has a day..
Things just don't go your way..
Some say fuck it! Come what may!.

Some days are meant for play..
Some days, in bed I stay..
Some days, I want what they
Say someday, will come my way..

Some days they say obey..
Some days I rebel, OK? OK!.
Some days, those who delay
Say someday, will go astray..

Some days I use hairspray..
Some days I turn to Tay..
Some days peeps on Sunday
Say someday, for me they'll pray..

11142023.01172024

In The Garden

One day she was wonderin' around
& saw a snake on the ground
who said 'come taste what I've found,
in the garden'!.

As she stepped her way closer
not knowin' life would be over
the second she did as he told her,
in the garden!.

She opened up her mouth & took a big bite,
now questioning if her decision was right!.
Will the fight in her head go on alllll night,
in the garden?.

Now she knows & she can't not know,
trapped in her head with nowhere to go!.
That's what she wanted, so she'll take the
blow,
in the fkn garden!.

There's no way out, she'll love forever,
no telling of time, it's now or never!.
She did the crime, fuck it, whatever,
in the garden!.

12172023.01172024

You Have Won

Writing my friends into their parts..
Who is to stay, which ones have hearts..

We are alllll standing here, center stage..
Not knowing if someone or you will turn
the page..

Alllll the happenings will go down in
history..
Alllll the kids will think life's a mystery..

But one can learn what it is really about..
& once you know, you'll know with no
doubt..

So learn the lessons & take the chances..
Life will always be full of questions..

When answers are found, it's a treasure, at
best..
Take them & share them with alllll the rest..

Only you can decide what to do with it..
Keep looking, don't you ever quit..

Eyes always wide-open, looking for clues..
Take notice, there's a difference in blues..

When the moon is high & your day is done..
You will then know, it is you who has won..

11032023.01172024

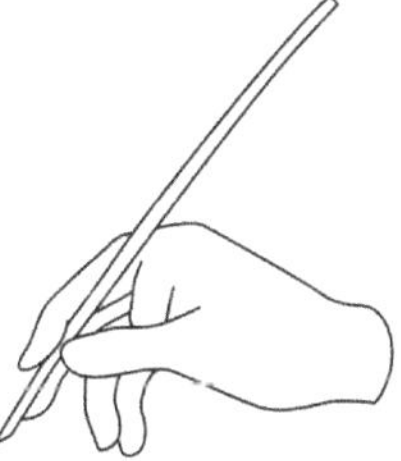

If You Ever Wanna Fuck Me

If you ever wanna fuck me..
Here's what you'll need to know..
Not everybody gets this key..
Listen up, I'll talk slow..

If the pace in mind is rapid..
I won't be down for it..
There is nothing fkn forbid..
Just slow it down a bit..

Remind me why I would want to..
Say 'fuck me' anyway..
Touch alllll of me, make me feel you..
You might just hear me say..

'Sir, are you tryin' to fuck me?.
I fkn knew you were..
BRB, I'll fkn go pee..
What makes you know for sure?.

I brought me back a black towel..
I'll try & stay on it..
When you do go on the prowl..
You will target my clit..

Your dick is hard AF..
Nothing like my soft touch..
This shit makes us stoopid & deaf..
It's alllll a 'lil tooo much..

But here you find me, in your bed..
Takin' it slow, got me alllll wet..
What would you rather do instead..
Of fuck me, then cigarette..

12022023.01212024

Why Do I Choose Fear?

Chin in hand..
Paper note on wall..
Crinkled words crying..
They trip, they fall..

Diamond shaped hands..
Eyes rest closed..
Sittin' on the bed..
No one knows..

Thoughts are colliding..
In the thick of it..
I can feel'em fighting..
Split, fuck this shit..

Nowhere to hide..
No place to go..
Lookin' around..
Who's eatin' crow..

Disgustedness lingers..
Disappointment awaits..
Which corner will it be around?.
What ghost holds our fate?.

Full moon's arising..
Bewitching hours are near..
What's that sign mean?.
Why do I choose fear?.

10002023.01172024

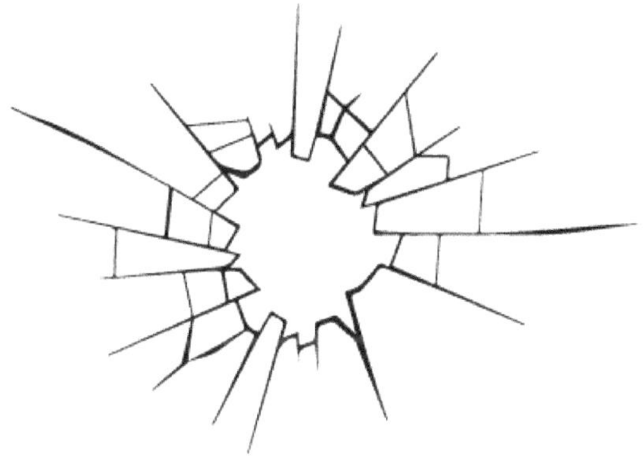

Cheatin'

He came up the stairs cryin'..
Said he had caught me lyin'..
He's done with alllll the tryin'..
My bullshit he ain't buyin'..

I fkd up big this time..
Crossed the brightest line..
Feelings intertwined..
Left me in a bind..

'I love him & I'm leavin'..
No need for your pleadin'..
I have a really good reason..
& know cheatin' is fkn treason..

'What are you gonna do?.
& who the fuck are you?.
I need you to be true..
My fks are down to few'..

'My heart is screaming ouch..
You can sleep on the couch..
I need to look in your pouch..
Stop being such a grouch'..

Nights & days go by..
We try & try & try..
Not sure if we'll be revived..
Or end up alllll sucked dry..

Cryin' tears of sadness..
Wantin' more of the madness..
Tryin' not to obsess..
This is alllll a fkn mess..

We think we're here for the long run..
We know at times it's fun..
This day might be done..
New comes with the setting sun..

11072023/12222023

Before Again

We did it before & we'll do it again..
I will be here until the end..
For you, for me, for us, for them..
Together forever, we're on the mend..

We are both stoopid, we are both strong..
Sometimes we don't know which way to
turn..
The smoke will be cleared before tooo long..
But the storm has come & fueled the burn..

We will get there, wherever there is..
Uphill is the battle but also the thrill..
Steppin' through the steps, hers & his..
Cause we both know how real love should
feel..

10232023

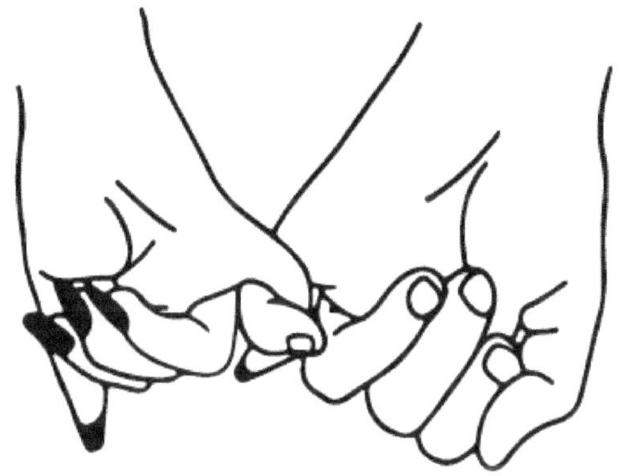

Afraid No More

Lessons will teach, when words cannot..
Once learned, never forgot..
Those life lessons, can not be bought..
Hold on tight, it's a lot..

As for now, the comfort is tossed..
Brave & bold, can't be lost..
Just be you, whatever lines crossed..
No matter what the cost..

You're gonna fall, you're gonna trip..
Maybe learn not to slip..
Create a way the script can flip..
Don't sink the fkn ship..

It is yours to take so rejoice..
There will be no invoice..
Protecting it is not a choice..
Speak now & use your voice..

Take these lessons & go explore..
Keep them close & you'll soar..
You're not hiding behind the door..
Not afraid anymore . . .

11022023

Reaching Out

Hitting the keys one by one..
Making sure alllll was done..

Softly crying just like she said..
I'm trying to put this alllll to bed..

Reachin' out to alllll the strangers..
Cause she knows alllll the dangers..

Tryin' to not let it arrange her..
But fuck these thoughts, they do derange her..

After hitting send there was an amend..
As she hoped for a friend to help her find the end..

11142023

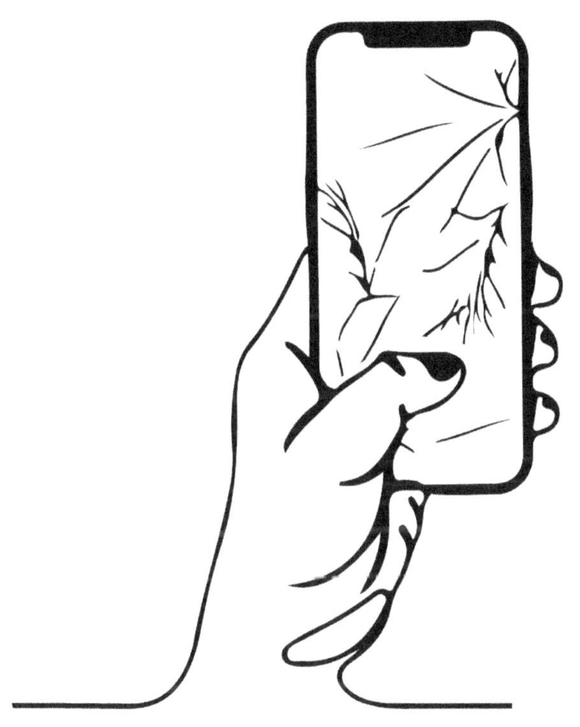

Scarlet Letter

So you say you wanna letter..
A scarlet one would be better..
So here's to you & here's to me..
Let's see if this is clever..

Dear sir, please take my hand..
Be kind, don't misunderstand..
My knees were weak, my mind was mush..
Meet me in Wonderland..

I'll love you now & then..
I'll love you till the end..
Forgive my deeds, change the plan..
We're more than just a trend..

If it works, then it works..
If it doesn't, we lose the perks..
Yet we try & try & try again..
Not knowing what evil lurks..

& now you wanna hear this..
Fuck alllll the reminisce..
Say you love me, say you want me..
& end this with a kiss!.

10162023

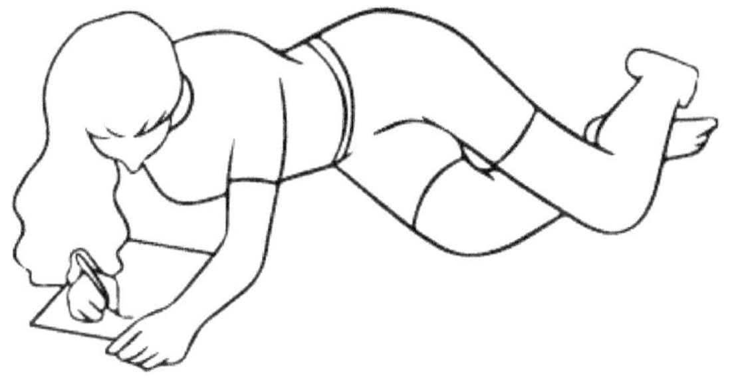

Who Brought The Pain

You asked in vain..
Who brought the pain?.
We both got to gain..
I'll try & explain..

We're not the same..
But you're not insane..
Stop alllll the playin'..
Hear what I'm sayin'?.

This life is to blame..
Got lost on the way..
What price will we pay..
To stay here today..

Well first there's the stain..
That came to defame..
Our family name..
We'll have to reclaim..

Next is to tame..
This nasty love game..
Put thoughts on a chain..
& a lid on the shame..

Gotta use your brain..
Abstain, refrain, restrain..
Stay til you obtain..
Injected novocaine..

One day you'll attain..
That love you want again..
Be sure to maintain..
Your love in the rain..

Life can be lame..
Keep fannin' the flame..
Get over the maim..
Now fkn proclaim..

*this is a reply to the original poem written to me . . . you
can find it in 'His Side of the Story'*

11142023

Help A Girl Out

Would ya, could ya, help a girl out?.
Point the way & I'll go..
Nowhere to be, no one to tell..
No way to know, what you don't know..

But once you know, you can't not know..
So hold on tight for now..
This is alllll gonna blow your mind..
Just please don't ask me how..

Look deep into those eyes, my dear..
You'll find the answers there..
That key has been there alllll along..
You were just unaware..

Don't break the stare that can be broken..
Just keep the gaze intact..
You will know when you see it..
You will know for a fact..

Hold on to what you know for sure..
Your fam, your friends, your man..
You may have fkd up big this time..
Strayed tooo far off the plan..

Forgive yourself, let them forgive..
Serve peace throughout the day..
Everything will work itself out..
Be patient. . . the fuck you say..

11022023

Who Are You?

So who are you? I have been asked,
Not your name, nor your role,
Not your memories from the past,
But the you in your soul..

How would one know who they now are?.
Should you ask your best friend?.
Or that someone in the mirror,
If you crack, will you mend?.

Go down, way down, til down is up,
Then ask yourself again,
So who are you? No more makeup,
& where the heck you been?.

I ask myself, out loud, sometimes,
What, where, when, why & how?.
Could I have done alllll of these crimes,
And still you want me now?.

Confused, I sit right by your side,
Up we go, down we come,
Not sure how to stay on this ride,
Why do I feel so dumb?.

Still not knowing the answer to,
The question, who are you?.
Hiding then seeking for the clue,
The one you can pursue..

I may be lost, can I be found?.
Is there a me to find?.
Who really knows, maybe I'm bound,
Tied up alllll in my mind..

I want me back, first & foremost,
Keep those eyes open wide,
If you happen to see my ghost,
It doesn't mean I died..

As I think my thoughts, I wander,
See shadows of my past,
Seeking whispers, hearing thunder,
Hoping truth is unmasked..

As I scan through files in my mind,
I see stories untold,
Pieces of me, I long to find,
Some new & some are old..

So who am I? The quest persists,
For me to find that key,
Unlocking doors where souls exists,
To rediscover me..

Lost, yet hopeful, I'm moving on,
In delicate design,
For in the search, I may be drawn,
To the essence that is mine..

11022023.01212024

In My Mind

Where are you? I am with who?.
Is it safe or was that a myth tooo?.

WTF is that? Nobody knows?.
Why don't I have on alllll my black clothes?.

I know, you know, we've been here before..
Familiar scatter alllll over the floor..

There is no order, nothing makes sense..
Just make a decision, get off the fence..

The pretty, the ugly, the bad, the good..
Alllll right in front of you, if you would..

Analyze it alllll, see what it's worth..
Maybe you'll have some sort of rebirth..

Alone is where you need to be?.
With alllll your thoughts & not with me..

I am here but where are you?.
Out there? In here? Neither of the two?.

What am I supposed to do?.
You still don't have a fkn clue?.

Tooo many thoughts passing through..
They fly by fast & they're not alllll true..

How will you ever figure it out?.
When you know, you'll know,
there will be no doubt!.

11042023.01182024

I Thought

I thought you said you knew me..
That you want to be true to me..
I could be whatever I wanna be..
& that was alllll OK, you see!.

Now a different pic is being painted..
Certain things should not be tainted..
Cried so hard I almost fainted..
This is just a big mess now, ain't it?.

IDGAF about plenty of things..
But when I get stuck, I want everything..
A need to know that always brings..
Fire to my ass, then the sirens sing..

Fuck alllll the bullshit, I got what I need..
Just gotta smoke a 'lil more weed..
Will these thoughts ever be freed?.
Isn't there a book I'm supposed to read?.

12212023.01192024

This Girl

in this world that's loud AF,
where conformiTy rEigns..
theRe's this girl who strolls
to her own refrAins..

not Like the others,
she stands apart..
a masterpiece of individuaLity,
a fkn work of art..

her spirit is a canvas,
painted dark & boLd..
a coLLecTion of stories,
waiting to be told..

witH Each step she steps,
she Breaks the mold..
she strUts with a uniqueness,
she's how oLd?.

in a garden of roses,
she's a rare bLoom..
a kaleidoScope of colors
cast alllll over tHe room..

her laughter, a melody,
so dIsTinct & clear..
a song only she knoWs,
she whIspers in your ear..

she wears her quirks
just Like a crown..
in a worLd that trieS
to bring HEr down..

her wordS, a beacon,
a guiding lighT..
a testament to courage
that's shIning bright..

her path is rocky,
intentionaLLy designed..
with every twist,
a discovery she finds..

not afraid anymore,
she will stand alone..
in her world,
authenticity is the throne..

emBracing thE exTraordinary,
in tHe mundane..
she weaves her web
on a vIbrant, bright terrain..

thiS GIRL is not like others,
still sharp as a tack..
FFS her way's the anthem,
that's a fact..

so here's to thIs girl,
who hears what they alllll say..
yet in this worlD of replicas,
she'll still do it her fKn way . . . .

01192024.01212024